THE
SECRET PLACE
WITHIN
Become "Very Good" Again

Leaders Guide

By: Craig Jemmott
4Given Life – Music Ministries, PLLC
© 2026

References

The Secret Place Within - Become "Very Good" Again Leader's Guide, Copyright © 2026, Craig Jemmott - 4Given Life Music Ministries, PLLC.

All Rights reserved. No portion of this Leaders Guide (containing text and references from the main readers book) may be reproduced, stored or transmitted in any form or by any means without prior consent of 4Given Life - Music Ministries, PLLC.

Scripture quotations marked NKJV are taken from the New King James Version. Copyright © 1982 by Thomas Nelson, Inc. Used by permission. All rights reserved.

Scripture quotations marked NLT are taken from the Holy Bible, New Living Translation. Copyright © 1996, 2004, 2015 by Tyndale House Foundation. Used by permission of Tyndale House Ministries, Carol Stream, Illinois 60188. All rights reserved.

Scripture quotations marked NIV are taken from the Holy Bible, *New International Version, NIV.* Copyright © 1973, 1978, 1984, by Biblica, Inc. Used by permission. All rights reserved worldwide.

Scripture quotations marked ESV are from The Holy Bible, English Standard Version, Copyright © 1982 by Crossway Bibles, a division of Good News Publishers. Used by permission. All Rights Reserved.

Scripture quotations marked GNT are taken from the Good News Translation in Today's English Version - Second Edition. Copyright 1992 American Bible Society. Used by permission.

Chapman, Gary D. *The Five Love Languages: The Secret to Love That Lasts.* Northfield Publishing, 2010.

Kingdom Dynamic: *New Birth, The Message of the Kingdom* (John 3:1-5), New Spirit Filled Life Bible, Copyright © 2002, Thomas

Nelson, Inc. Used by permission of HarperCollins Christian Publishing.

Nee, Watchman. *The Combination of the Soul and the Flesh*. Bible Portal - sermon message.

Definitions are taken from: Webster's New 20th Century 2nd Edition, 1958, World Publishing Company.
Oxford Languages, 2025 and Miriam-Webster.com, 2025.

Book Cover: Designed by author on Canva and recreated via Adobe InDesign. Cover Image of the door originally painted by Matti Jemmott.

Author's Note: This Leader's Guide was prayerfully developed as a companion to the workbook and the original reader's book. AI tools were used to assist with organizing and formatting content, but all material was reviewed, refined, and expanded by the author. The added leader tips, discussion prompts, and practical helps were created through study, prayer, and discernment. While technology supported the process, the heart, biblical foundation, and creative direction of this guide come from the author under the leading of the Holy Spirit.

Disclaimer: This material is intended for spiritual growth, education, and personal reflection. The author is not a licensed counselor, therapist, or medical professional. The content herein is not designed to diagnose, treat, or cure any physical, emotional, or mental health condition.
Readers and participants are encouraged to seek appropriate professional help when needed. If you are facing emotional, mental, or physical health challenges, please consult a qualified healthcare or counseling professional.
The insights and practices shared here are offered in good faith for your encouragement and growth. How you choose to use them is your responsibility. The author and publisher cannot be held liable for personal outcomes.

ISBN: 979-8-9927492-3-6

Contents

References..2
Contents...4
   Introduction to the Leader's Guide......................................7
How to Use This Leader's Guide..9
Emotional Care Guidelines — Leaders Guide........................13
Group Rules & Guidelines..18
The Purpose of Repetition in Reflection Questions................21
Session / Meeting Flow..25
Section 1 — Scientific & Biblical Truth....................................28
      Section Overview (Leader's Notes).............................28
      Preparation for Leaders...29
      Facilitation Tips..29
      Leader's Note: Daily & Weekly Activities....................30
      Sample Discussion Questions.....................................31
      Leader's Encouragement Note....................................31
      Optional Add-Ons..32
Section 2 — Idols / Other Gods (Attachments)........................33
      Section Overview (Leader's Notes).............................33
      Preparation for Leaders...34
      Facilitation Tips..34
      Sample Discussion Questions.....................................34
      Leader's Encouragement Note....................................35
      Optional Add-Ons..35
      Deliverance Prayers for Group Use (Leader's Guide)...........36
Section 3 — Belief System..37
      Section Overview (Leader's Notes).............................38
      Preparation for Leaders...39
      Facilitation Tips..39
      Emotional Care & Safety..40
      Sample Discussion Questions.....................................40

    Leader's Encouragement Note..41
    Optional Add-Ons..41
    Deliverance Prayers (Optional)..41

Section 4 — My Battle: Offenses, Resentments, Bitterness & Healing..43
    Section Overview (Leader's Notes).....................................43
    Preparation for Leaders..44
    Facilitation Tips..44
    Emotional Care & Safety..45
    Sample Discussion Questions..45
    Leader's Encouragement Note..46
    Optional Add-Ons..46
    Deliverance Prayers (Optional)..46

Section 5 — Soul, Flesh & Spirit...48
    Section Overview (Leader's Notes).....................................48
    Preparation for Leaders..49
    Facilitation Tips..49
    Emotional Care & Safety..49
    Sample Discussion Questions..50
    Leader's Encouragement Note..50
    Optional Add-Ons..51
    Deliverance Prayers (Optional)..51

Section 6 — The New Man..52
    Section Overview (Leader's Notes).....................................53
    Preparation for Leaders..54
    Facilitation Tips..54
    Emotional Care & Safety..54
    Sample Discussion Questions..55
    Leader's Encouragement Note..55
    Optional Add-Ons..55

Section 7 — Walk in the Spirit..57
    Section Overview (Leader's Notes).....................................57
    Preparation for Leaders..58

    Facilitation Tips.. 58
    Emotional Care & Safety... 58
    Sample Discussion Questions.. 59
    Leader's Encouragement Note... 59
    Optional Add-Ons.. 60
    Prayer & Commitment... 60

Section 8 — My Testimony.. 62
    Section Overview (Leader's Notes)....................................... 62
    Preparation for Leaders:.. 63
    Facilitation Tips:.. 63
    Emotional Care & Safety... 63
    Sample Discussion Questions:... 64
    Leader's Encouragement Note:.. 64
    Optional Add-Ons.. 64
    Prayer & Commitment... 65

Section 9 — A Transformed Heart.. 67
    Section Overview (Leader's Notes)....................................... 67
    Preparation for Leaders:.. 68
    Facilitation Tips:.. 68
    Emotional Care & Safety... 68
    Sample Discussion Questions:... 69
    Leader's Encouragement Note:.. 69
    Optional Add-Ons.. 70
    Prayer & Commitment... 71

Section 10 — 30, 60, 100 Fold.. 72
    Section Overview (Leader's Notes)....................................... 72
    Preparation for Leaders... 73
    Facilitation Tips... 74
    Emotional Care & Safety... 74
    Sample Discussion Questions.. 76
    Optional Add-Ons for Leaders... 76
    Leader's Encouragement Note... 77

Prayer & Commitment... 77
Extending the Journey: The Secret Place Within Ecosystem. 79
Final Conclusion — No Longer a Secret Place.............................81
    Section Overview (Leader's Notes)....................................... 81
    Preparation for Leaders:... 82
    Facilitation Tips:...82
    Emotional Care & Safety.. 83
    Sample Discussion Questions:...83
    Optional Add-Ons... 84
    Prayer & Commitment.. 84
The Journey's End — Wrap-Up & Stepping Forward in the Spirit...... 86
    Section Overview (Leader's Notes)....................................... 86
    Final Checklist – Walking It Out..86
    Encouragement for the Journey Ahead................................87
    S.T.A.N.D — Support Team Accountability Network Defense...... 87
    Leader's Encouragement Note...88

Introduction to the Leader's Guide

Welcome to the **Leader's Guide** for this transformative workbook. This guide is designed to equip you, as a leader, facilitator, or mentor, to shepherd participants through a journey of renewal, freedom, and Spirit-led living. While the workbook focuses on personal reflection, journaling, and Scripture engagement, the Leader's Guide adds depth, structure, and practical tools to help participants process and apply these truths in real life.

As a leader, your role is not to have all the answers, but to create a safe, Spirit-filled environment where participants can explore their thoughts, confront struggles, and experience God's transformative work. Your guidance will help participants integrate biblical principles, neuroscientific insights, and spiritual practices into daily life, moving from understanding to action.

Note for Leaders: Participants will be following a 7-day rhythm in their workbook each week: Scripture Engagement, Truth Connection, Neuroscience Meets Scripture, Application Challenge, My Story, Freedom Moment, and Rest. Keep this rhythm in mind as you prepare and pace your sessions.

How to Use This Leader's Guide

This guide is structured to correspond with the workbook's 11 sections, plus the final wrap-up. Here's how to get the most out of it:

1. Preparation Before Each Session

- **Pray**: Ask for the Holy Spirit's guidance, wisdom, and sensitivity to participants' needs.
- **Review Scripture and Notes**: Familiarize yourself with the key verses, reflection questions, and optional add-ons.
- **Prepare Materials**: Ensure journals, pens, charts, and any handouts are ready.

2. Facilitation Tips

- **Encourage Reflection**: Ask open-ended questions to help participants think deeply.
- **Neuroscience Tie-In**: When appropriate, highlight how the brain interacts with habits, thought patterns, and spiritual growth.
- **Practical Exercises**: Use analogies, small group discussions, or guided activities to reinforce concepts.
- **Celebrate Progress**: Recognize small wins and Spirit-led choices to motivate participants.

3. Maintaining Emotional & Spiritual Safety

- Some sections explore sensitive areas like past struggles, shame, or trauma.
- Encourage participants to journal privately, seek prayer support, and engage accountability partners.

- Remind participants that transformation is a process, not perfection.

4. Session Structure

Each workbook section is mirrored in this guide for leadership facilitation:

- **Section Overview**: Explains the purpose and key goal of the session.
- **Preparation for Leaders**: Notes, Scripture, and materials to review.
- **Facilitation Tips**: Guidance on leading discussion, exercises, and reflection.
- **Discussion Questions**: To spark meaningful dialogue.
- **Optional Add-Ons**: Ideas to deepen engagement for participants ready to go further.
- **Prayer & Commitment**: Includes suggested prayers and prompts for personal commitment.
- **Leader Encouragement Note**: Key reminders for supporting participants in the Spirit.

Note: Please see the "Session / Meeting Flow" on page 25.

5. Encouraging Ongoing Growth

- At the conclusion of the workbook, participants are guided to reflect on their journey, commit to daily practices, and establish accountability networks.
- Leaders are encouraged to help participants set goals, track progress, and celebrate victories as they step forward in the Spirit.

6. Flexibility

- Use this guide as a framework, not a script. Adjust discussions, exercises, or timing based on your group's needs.
- Some participants may move faster or slower; provide extra space for journaling, prayer, or personal reflection as needed.

Note for Leaders:
Participants will be following a 7-day rhythm in their workbook each week: Scripture Engagement, Truth Connection, Neuroscience Meets Scripture, Application Challenge, My Story, Freedom Moment, and Rest. Keep this rhythm in mind as you prepare and pace your sessions.

Leader Safety Note: Supporting Trauma-Affected Participants

This study may touch sensitive areas of people's stories. As a leader, your role is not to be a therapist but to create a safe, grace-filled environment. Keep these principles in mind:

1. **Honor Choice:** Always give participants permission to "pass" or skip a question. Never pressure someone to share more than they want to.

2. **Watch for Signs of Overload:** If someone becomes tearful, anxious, or withdrawn, pause and offer a break. Remind them they can step outside, journal quietly, or simply listen.

3. **Use Grounding Tools:** Encourage the "90-Second Grounding Exercise" (naming things they see, touch,

hear, smell, breathing slowly) if emotions spike.

4. **Refer, Don't Counsel:** If deep trauma or crisis surfaces, gently affirm them and encourage professional support. Leaders are companions, not clinicians.

5. **Close in Safety:** Always end group sessions with prayer, scripture, or a calming reflection so participants leave feeling anchored, not raw.

Remember: Your role is to facilitate a safe, Spirit-led environment for exploration and growth. Trust God to work through both you and the participants. Focus on encouragement, reflection, and application, guiding participants to live in the truth, power, and freedom of Christ.

Emotional Care Guidelines — Leaders Guide

Use this leader version when facilitating any workbook session that may surface painful memories or strong emotions. Read it before every session and share the short **Leader's Opening** (pg. 17) with the group at the start. This version keeps the original participant wording but adds practical cues, scripts, and leader actions so you can shepherd the group safely and compassionately.

---

1. Safety First (for leaders)

Core guidance for facilitators

- Remind the group: *Pause when overwhelmed. Strong emotions are normal.* Encourage participants to stop the exercise if they become uncomfortable.
- Offer alternatives: participants may journal, pray, draw, or sit quietly instead of sharing.
- Know your limits: you are a leader, not a therapist. If someone needs more than pastoral support, refer them to a mental-health professional.
- Confidentiality: establish and enforce a "what's shared here stays here" agreement.

Leader actions

- Before the session: post a small sign with local crisis numbers and any logistics (break room, restroom, quiet space).
- During the session: watch body language (shaking,

dissociation, withdrawal). If someone appears triggered, gently offer a break or a one-on-one check-in.
- After the session: allow 5–10 minutes of light, restoring activity (prayer, song, guided breathing) to bring emotional regulation before people leave.

---

2. Grounding Tool: 90 Seconds to Calm — with Prayer

Teach both sensory grounding and short prayer practices so participants have spiritual and somatic tools.

90-Second Grounding Tool (teach & model):

1. Name **5 things you can see** (pause).
2. Name **4 things you can touch** (pause).
3. Name **3 things you can hear** (pause).
4. Name **2 things you can smell** (pause).
5. Take **3 slow breaths** (in for 4, out for 6).

Add prayer as grounding (two quick options):

- **Breath Prayer:** Inhale slowly and silently say, *"Lord, You are with me."* Exhale and say, *"I release this to You."* Repeat 3 times.
- **Scripture Prayer:** Lead the group in a short verse (example): *"Cast all your cares on Him, for He cares for you." (1 Peter 5:7)* — read together, then pause.

Leader tip: Demonstrate the grounding aloud once. Invite participants to use either the sensory or prayer version (or both) whenever they feel triggered.

3. How to Engage Each Section Safely (leader prompts & options)

Use these leader cues when introducing each workbook section:

- **Scripture Engagement** – Prompt: *"Read slowly. Notice what feels comforting and what feels hard. Focus on the phrase that brings peace."* Offer the option to journal privately.
- **Truth Connection** – Prompt: *"Compare a painful belief with Scripture. Invite small, testable actions rather than immediate 'fixes.'"* Encourage attendees to choose gentle experiments.
- **Neuroscience Meets Scripture** – Briefly explain (simple language) how feelings and memory can replay offenses; pair each teaching point with a 60–90 second calming practice.
- **Application Challenge** – Offer three tiers (light / moderate / deeper). Example prompt: *"Choose the level that keeps you safe—no pressure."*
- **My Story** – Make sharing explicitly optional. Provide formats: 1) silent journaling, 2) written bullet points, 3) short verbal share (max 2 minutes).
- **Freedom Moment** – Lead a short, simple ritual (breath prayer, holding a stone, symbolic release). Keep symbolism limited so it's not triggering.
- **Closing Challenge & Celebration** – Focus on small wins. Invite one line of testimony or a short gratitude sentence; never require detail.

4. Group Guidelines (for facilitators to set and enforce)

- **Optional sharing:** Repeat at the start: *"No one is required to disclose painful details."*
- **Confidentiality & respect:** Remind participants to protect privacy and avoid unsolicited advice.
- **Signal system:** Offer a discreet way to indicate distress (e.g., raise a hand or step outside).
- **Time & pacing:** Don't rush. Keep a predictable rhythm: teaching → quiet reflection → grounding → short discussion.
- **Referral plan:** Have a list of local counselors, clergy, and crisis lines to offer when needed.

---

5. Crisis & Support Plan (leader responsibilities)

- If someone is in immediate danger, call **911 (U.S.)**.
- If someone expresses suicidal intent or imminent harm, stay with them, call emergency services, and follow your organization's safety protocol.
- National Crisis Lifeline (U.S.): **988** — keep this visible to the group.
- Maintain private notes (confidential) of any safety concerns and follow up personally with the participant afterward.
- Optional - Provide a blank area on printed handouts or a slide to add local/faith-based or professional contact information.

Quick Leader's Opening (read this verbatim or adapt)

> "Welcome. A quick note before we begin: this material may touch tender areas of your story. If you feel overwhelmed at any time, you are free to pause, step out, or use the 90-second grounding practice we will do together. Sharing is optional; confidentiality and kindness are expected. If you need more support, I'll share referral options at the end. Let's take a breath together." *(Lead the 90-Second Grounding with Breath Prayer once.)*

Remember: This workbook is a tool for growth, not a substitute for therapy. Move at your pace. Celebrate every step.

Remind participants that their workbook includes Emotional Care Guidelines (see pg. 11). Encourage them to review it regularly and use the 90-Second Reset if needed.

Group Rules & Guidelines

Purpose: To create a safe, supportive, and Spirit-led environment for all participants.

1. Confidentiality

- What is shared in the group stays in the group.
- Respect the privacy of others; do not share stories, struggles, or personal information outside the group without permission.

2. Respectful Communication

- Listen without interrupting.
- Speak kindly and avoid judgment or criticism.
- Allow everyone to have a voice; don't dominate discussion.

3. Participation & Engagement

- Be present and participate actively.
- Complete daily and weekly activities as able.
- Share your thoughts, reflections, and insights honestly, but only as you feel comfortable.

4. Spiritual Sensitivity

- Honor differences in spiritual experiences or expressions.
- Encourage one another with Scripture and prayer.
- Avoid debating personal beliefs; focus on shared growth and understanding.

5. Safe Environment

- Be aware of emotional triggers; respect personal boundaries.
- If a topic is too sensitive, it's okay to step out or take a break.
- Leaders are available for guidance and prayer support if needed.

6. Accountability

- Commit to attending regularly and tracking personal progress.
- Partner with an accountability buddy if desired for encouragement and prayer.
- Share victories and struggles responsibly, supporting one another in obedience to God.

7. Group Norms for Discussion

- Use "I" statements: speak about your own experience, not others'.
- Avoid giving unsolicited advice; offer encouragement

instead.
- Keep discussions solution-focused and Spirit-centered.

8. Prayer & Confidential Support

- Respect each participant's level of comfort with prayer.
- Offer prayer when asked, but never force prayer participation.
- Leaders may provide one-on-one support for sensitive topics.

9. Commitment to Growth

- Approach the workbook and group with a teachable heart.
- Celebrate progress, even small steps, as victories in God's Kingdom.
- Remember: transformation is a journey; encourage patience and consistency.

Leader Reminders:

- Model confidentiality, respect, and Spirit-led guidance.
- Check in with participants regularly to ensure emotional safety.
- Reinforce that the group is a supportive environment, not a counseling session.

The Purpose of Repetition in Reflection Questions

Overview

As a leader, you'll notice that many reflection questions throughout the workbook sound similar — for example:

- "When has your flesh felt stronger than your spirit?"
- "How do you know when you're walking in the Spirit versus the flesh?"
- "What lie have you believed about yourself in the past?"
- "How has God brought freedom in this area?"

This repetition is not redundancy — it's reinforcement by design. Each repeated theme is part of a transformational rhythm that integrates biblical renewal and brain retraining.

---

1. Neuroscience: Repetition Builds Renewal

The brain changes through repetition. Every time a participant revisits a similar question, they are strengthening new neural pathways aligned with truth.

- Old pathways (limbic/flesh patterns) fade through lack of use.
- New pathways (prefrontal/Spirit-led patterns) grow stronger through reflection, journaling, and prayer.

Each recurring question helps participants replace reactive habits with Spirit-led decision-making.

"Be transformed by the renewing of your mind." – Romans 12:2

Repetition literally rewires the mind — spiritually and neurologically.

---

2. Spiritual Formation: Reflection → Conviction → Transformation

Scripture repeats truth because transformation requires meditation, not just information.

- In the same way, your participants need repeated opportunities to revisit their identity, freedom, and spiritual growth.
- The same question asked at a different stage produces a deeper answer.
    - Early in the workbook: awareness.
    - Midway: conviction and surrender.
    - Later: testimony and transformation.

Repetition allows participants to *see* how far they've come — it becomes living evidence of sanctification.

3. Discipleship: Repetition Creates Rhythm and Safety

For participants healing from trauma or deep habits, predictability builds safety.

- Familiar formats and recurring prompts lower anxiety and increase engagement.
- Leaders can focus less on "explaining" and more on *listening* and *supporting*.
- The repetition signals to participants: "You're still on the journey — and it's okay to take another pass through this layer."

This consistent rhythm mirrors the grace of God — patient, steady, and renewing.

---

4. Facilitator Practice: How to Use Repetition Intentionally

- Highlight Growth: Ask, "How is your answer different from when you saw a similar question earlier?"
- Encourage Journaling: Have participants re-read earlier entries to see evidence of renewal.
- Normalize Process: Remind them that maturity happens layer by layer — not all at once.
- Connect the Dots: Use repetition to show how one section builds on another (e.g., lies → identity → freedom → new man → Spirit-led life).

5. Summary for Leaders

Purpose for Repetition	Effect
Reinforces neural and spiritual renewal	Strengthens truth-based thinking
Creates safe, familiar rhythm	Reduces anxiety and fosters openness
Shows visible growth over time	Builds measurable transformation
Simplifies group facilitation	Keeps flow consistent for leaders

---

Leader Encouragement

> "Repetition isn't boring — it's sacred.
> Each familiar question gives the Holy Spirit another chance to rewrite the story.
> Stay faithful to the process, and watch participants move from awareness to freedom to transformation."

Session / Meeting Flow

This guide is designed to provide a clear, consistent flow for each session while still allowing space for the Holy Spirit to lead.
Leaders are encouraged to follow the rhythm below, adjusting timing as needed for their group.

Recommended Flow for Each Session

1. Welcome & Connection

- Greet participants and create a calm, welcoming atmosphere
- Brief informal check-in (no pressure to share deeply)
- Remind the group of confidentiality and emotional safety

2. Opening Prayer

- Pray either the section-specific opening prayer, provided in this guide, or your own prayer.
- Invite God's presence, peace, and truth into the session
- Set a tone of grace, not performance

3. Review & Grounding (Optional but Encouraged)

- Briefly remind participants:
    - There is no "behind" or "ahead"

- - Daily activities change; weekly activities continue
- Invite a short grounding moment (pause, breath, prayer)

4. Teaching Focus

- Introduce the main theme of the section
- Highlight key truths or concepts (Scripture, framework, insight)
- Keep teaching concise and accessible
- Avoid correcting or "fixing" participants during this time

5. Group Discussion

- Use the provided discussion questions
- Encourage sharing without pressure to disclose personal trauma
- Affirm participation; silence is acceptable
- Gently redirect if discussion becomes advice-giving or judgmental

6. Activity Review & Clarification

- Briefly reference:
  - Daily Activities (day-specific)
  - Weekly Activities (ongoing)
- Clarify expectations and answer logistical questions
- Remind participants that awareness matters more than completion

7. Reflection or Quiet Processing

- Allow time for journaling, silence, or personal reflection
- Normalize different processing styles (speaking, writing, quiet)
- Do not rush this moment

8. Encouragement & Closing Direction

- Offer a short word of encouragement or summary truth
- Point participants toward the upcoming days in the workbook
- Reinforce grace, safety, and steady growth

9. Closing Prayer

- Thank God for what was shared and what is still unfolding
- Ask for peace, protection, and continued guidance during the week

Section 1 — Scientific & Biblical Truth

Opening Prayer

Father God, we come before You with open hearts and willing minds.
We invite Your presence into this space and ask that You establish safety, truth, and grace among us.
Help us to slow down, to be honest, and to listen — not only to one another, but to You.
Remove pressure, comparison, and fear, and replace them with peace and clarity.
We give You permission to lead this journey, trusting that You desire wholeness for each of us.
In Jesus' name, amen.

Section Overview (Leader's Notes)

This section introduces participants to the integration of science and Scripture. It explores how God designed the mind, highlighting the Spirit (prefrontal cortex) and the Soul (limbic system). Leaders should emphasize that both scientific insight and biblical revelation affirm God's wisdom in human design, and that old patterns can be transformed through renewing the mind.

Key Goal for Participants:
To understand the biblical and scientific framework of the mind and begin practicing Spirit-led decision making.

Preparation for Leaders

- Pray for participants to experience safety, curiosity, and openness in exploring science and Scripture together.
- Review 1 Corinthians 16:15, Genesis 1:31, Romans 12:2, Galatians 5:16–17.
- Familiarize yourself with the Spirit vs. flesh (prefrontal cortex vs. limbic system) chart.
- Materials: Bibles, journals, pens, optional whiteboard for Spirit vs. flesh examples.

Facilitation Tips

- **Create Emotional Safety:** Remind the group that some may connect this teaching to personal struggles with addiction, habits, or trauma. Normalize that this is a safe space.
- **Encourage Curiosity:** Invite participants to see the harmony between science and Scripture as evidence of God's wisdom.
- **Pacing:** Aim to spend time on both the biblical foundation and the practical reflection activities.
- **Group Sharing:** Use open-ended questions but give permission for participants to pass if they're not ready to share.

Leader's Note: Daily & Weekly Activities

Every day within each section, participants will be introduced to a Daily Activity, Weekly Activity or both. These activities are cumulative, not one-time assignments. (Explained on pg. 10-11 of the participants "Study Guide/Workbook".

When a new activity is introduced, participants are not expected to stop the previous one. Each activity carries forward into the following weeks, gently building a sustainable rhythm of growth.

How to Explain This to the Group

You may say:

> "Daily & Weekly Activities are meant to layer, not replace one another.
> You are not behind if you miss a day, and you are not failing if something feels difficult."

> "Progress in this study is measured by awareness, not perfection."

Emotional Safety Reminder

If a participant feels overwhelmed, encourage them to pause — not quit.

They may:

- Slow the activity down
- Focus on one activity for a season
- Return to an activity that feels grounding

Growth happens best in safety, not pressure.

Leader Tone to Maintain

- Normalize grace and flexibility
- Avoid comparison language
- Reinforce that transformation takes time

A participant keeping even one activity consistently is still experiencing success.

Sample Discussion Questions

- When you hear the word "addicted," what emotions or images come up for you?
- How does knowing God originally made you "very good" reframe the way you see yourself today?
- Where do you personally notice the "battle" between Spirit and flesh in your daily life?
- What's one "very good" choice you've made this week that reflects Spirit-led decision making?

Leader's Encouragement Note

As you guide this section, remember: participants may wrestle with old thought patterns or shame around past decisions.

Affirm often: *"God calls you very good. You are not defined by your old loops—you are defined by Christ's Spirit at work in you."* Watch for breakthrough moments when someone recognizes a new Spirit-led choice. Pause and celebrate these aloud.

Optional Add-Ons

- **Worship:** Open with a song about renewal or transformation (e.g., "Renew My Mind" themes).
- **Testimony Time:** Invite one person to share how God has helped them shift from old patterns to Spirit-led living.
- **Creative Exercise:** Have participants draw two circles—one labeled "flesh/limbic" and one "Spirit/prefrontal." Ask them to list what typically flows from each, then pray for God to strengthen their Spirit-led choices.

Closing Prayer for Leaders to Use with Group

"Father, we thank You for designing our minds and souls with wisdom. We repent of letting emotions and fleshly desires control us, and we renounce the lies that say we are bound to old patterns. We invite Your Holy Spirit to renew our minds and empower our choices. Seal this truth with the blood of Jesus, and help us walk in freedom. In Christ's name, Amen."

Section 2 — Idols / Other Gods (Attachments)

Opening Prayer

Lord, You alone are our source of life and security.
As we reflect on attachments and coping patterns, we ask for honesty and compassion toward ourselves and others.
Show us where we have leaned on things that cannot truly sustain us.
Help us release what competes with trust in You and guide us into freedom, not shame.
We welcome Your gentle correction and loving care.
In Jesus' name, amen.

Section Overview (Leader's Notes)

This section helps participants identify and release idols or "attachments" that take God's place in their lives. Idols can be relationships, habits, possessions, or even thought patterns. Leaders should guide gently, since attachments often come from wounds, unmet needs, or trauma.

Key Goal for Participants:
To recognize and surrender unhealthy attachments, exchanging false identities for God's truth and experiencing deeper devotion to Him.

Preparation for Leaders

- Pray for discernment and sensitivity, as conversations may touch painful or vulnerable areas.
- Review Zechariah 10:2, Galatians 4:8–9, Exodus 20:3–5, Luke 12:15, Jeremiah 31:3, 1 Samuel 16:7.
- Familiarize yourself with the "Attachments / False Identity / Truth of God's Word" chart.
- Materials: Bibles, journals, pens, optional worship music for reflection and closing celebration.

Facilitation Tips

- **Create Emotional Safety:** Remind participants they may pause, step back, or pray quietly if they feel overwhelmed. Safety comes before completion.
- **Normalize Struggle:** Frame attachments as a common human issue — not shame, but an invitation to freedom.
- **Encourage Small Steps:** Help participants celebrate even one surrendered attachment. God works gently and progressively.
- **Prayer Sensitivity:** Allow participants to choose whether to pray the gentle or authoritative deliverance prayer. Never pressure.

Sample Discussion Questions

- Why do you think God begins the Ten Commandments with "no other gods before Me"?

- In your life, what modern "attachments" could become idols if left unchecked?
- How have you seen an attachment create a false identity in your life or in culture?
- What truth from God's Word can replace that false identity?

Leader's Encouragement Note

Some participants may feel guilt or shame when they recognize idols in their lives. Gently remind them: *"God reveals idols not to condemn you, but to free you. Every act of release creates more room for His joy, peace, and love."*
Celebrate vulnerability in the group — even small confessions or insights are breakthroughs.

Optional Add-Ons

- **Worship:** Begin or close with a song of devotion (focus on God as "enough").
- **Testimony Time:** Invite someone to share how God freed them from an attachment.
- **Creative Exercise:** Ask participants to write their attachment on paper, then cross it out and write God's truth beside it. End with prayer.

Deliverance Prayers for Group Use (Leader's Guide)

Gentle Prayer of Release (new believers or tender hearts):
"Lord Jesus, I confess that I have held onto attachments that have taken Your place in my life. I repent for allowing them to shape my heart and identity. Today, I surrender them to You. I renounce the power they have had over me, and I invite Your Holy Spirit to fill the empty places with Your love and peace. Seal me with Your blood, Jesus, and guard my heart with Your truth. In the Mighty name of Jesus, I pray, Amen."

Authoritative Prayer of Breaking Idols and Attachments (mature believers):
"In the mighty name of Jesus Christ, I repent for allowing idols and attachments such as: _____ to rule in my life. I renounce every false god, every unhealthy attachment, and every false identity connected to them. I break their hold over me right now by the blood of Jesus. I declare that Jesus Christ is Lord over my heart, mind, and body. Holy Spirit, take full residence in me and restore my devotion to God alone. I seal this prayer in the blood of Jesus, and I claim my freedom in Him. In Jesus' Mighty name, I pray, Amen."

Leader Tip: Before dismissing, encourage participants to complete their daily/weekly activities and journaling prompts. Ask 1–2 volunteers to share insights from the past week to reinforce accountability.

Closing Prayer for Leaders to Use with Group

"Lord, thank You for lovingly revealing the attachments that try to take Your place. We repent for elevating them above You, and we release them into Your hands. Fill every space with Your Spirit, restore our devotion to You alone, and let our identity rest securely in Christ. Seal this freedom with the blood of Jesus. Amen."

Summary Theme

Releasing idols and attachments leads to true freedom and rest in God alone.

Section 3 — Belief System

Opening Prayer

Father, You are the God of truth.
As we begin this time, we ask You to gently reveal anything that has distorted how we think, believe, or see ourselves.
Give us discernment without condemnation and awareness without overwhelm.
Help us to recognize lies for what they are and to receive Your truth with humility and hope.
Lead us safely and patiently as You renew our minds.
In Jesus' name, amen.

Section Overview (Leader's Notes)

This section explores how both spoken lies from others and reactive lies we tell ourselves can form false belief systems—deeply rooted patterns stored in the limbic system that influence thoughts, emotions, and behaviors. Leaders should emphasize that God, through His Word and the guidance of the Holy Spirit, can reveal the truth, restore perspective, and empower participants to replace lies with Spirit-led beliefs. Participants will be invited to examine beliefs they have accepted, recognize falsehoods, and embrace the truth that sets them free.

Key Goal for Participants:
To recognize false belief systems, understand how they shape identity and behavior, and begin replacing lies with God's truth.

Preparation for Leaders

- Pray for participants to experience safety, courage, and openness in identifying false beliefs.
- Review John 8:44, Romans 12:2, Ephesians 1:4–7, Psalm 139:14, 2 Corinthians 5:17.
- Prepare materials: Bibles, journals, pens, optional whiteboard or chart for False Belief → Scripture Truth exercises.

Facilitation Tips

- **Create Emotional Safety:** Some participants may revisit painful lies or past trauma. Normalize pauses and private reflection.
- **Encourage Curiosity:** Emphasize the alignment of neuroscience (limbic memory vs. prefrontal cortex) and Scripture in reshaping beliefs.
- **Pacing:** Guide participants through reflection, journaling, and group discussion, allowing time for prayer and insight.
- **Group Sharing:** Encourage open-ended sharing but allow participants to pass if not ready.

Emotional Care & Safety

Why Here?
False beliefs often come from painful words, rejection, abuse, or abandonment. Confronting them can stir deep emotions.

Safety Note:
If memories surface while identifying lies, participants may pause, journal privately, pray, or seek a safe mentor. Emphasize that God works layer by layer.

Optional Reflection Exercise:

- Write one lie that feels safe to face today.
- Write one truth from Scripture that counters it.
- Pray: *"Holy Spirit, give me courage to face lies and anchor me in Your truth."*

Sample Discussion Questions

- What does it mean that Satan is called "the father of lies" (John 8:44)?
- How do lies influence our view of God, ourselves, and others?
- Why can lies feel believable at first?
- What is one lie you've believed about yourself in the past?
- How does recognizing a lie as false begin to break its power?

Leader's Encouragement Note

Remind participants:
"Lies may have shaped your past, but they do not define your future. Every time you name a lie and replace it with God's truth, you weaken the enemy's grip. Freedom comes step by step — and God celebrates each moment of surrender."

Optional Add-Ons

- **Worship:** Include a song about freedom, identity, or truth (e.g., "Who You Say I Am").
- **Creative Exercise:** Draw a chart linking False Belief → Emotional Reaction → Scripture Truth → New Response.
- **Testimony Time:** Invite participants to share a breakthrough in rejecting a lie and embracing God's truth.

Deliverance Prayers (Optional)

Gentle Prayer (Tender Hearts):
"Lord Jesus, I repent for believing lies about myself, others, and even about You. I renounce every false belief and identity shaped apart from Your truth. I invite Your Holy Spirit to renew my mind and fill me with Your Word. Wash me and seal me with the blood of Jesus. I choose to believe what You say about me. In Your Mighty name we pray, Amen."

Authoritative Prayer (Mature Believers):
"In the name of Jesus Christ, I repent for agreeing with the following lies and false belief systems: _____. I renounce every deception, spoken lie, and reactive lie. I cancel their power by the blood of Jesus. I declare I am who God says I am — loved, chosen, and free. Holy Spirit, replace every false system with unshakable truth. I seal this in the blood of Jesus. Amen."

Leader Tip: Before dismissing, encourage participants to complete their daily/weekly activities and journaling prompts. Ask 1–2 volunteers to share insights from the past week to reinforce accountability.

Closing Prayer for Leaders

"Lord, I thank You for exposing the false beliefs and lies that once shaped our lives. Help us stand on Your truth and reject every deception of the enemy. Replace every counterfeit thought with Your promises and let our minds be renewed daily. We celebrate Your truth and rest in Your love. In Jesus' name, Amen."

Summary Theme

Replacing lies with God's truth dismantles false belief systems and anchors our lives in freedom.

Section 4 — My Battle: Offenses, Resentments, Bitterness & Healing

Opening Prayer

Father, You are near to the brokenhearted.
As we enter this section, we ask for Your protection, wisdom, and peace.
Where there has been offense, pain, or unresolved hurt, lead us with patience and care.
Help us forgive as You lead — not by force, but by truth and grace.
Bring healing where it is needed and rest where hearts feel weary.
In Jesus' name, amen.

Section Overview (Leader's Notes)

This section helps participants recognize how offenses, resentment, and bitterness can leave emotional and spiritual scars. Leaders will guide participants to process and release these burdens through forgiveness and God's truth. Healing begins when participants intentionally allow the Holy Spirit to transform pain into freedom and peace.

Key Goal for Participants:
To identify unresolved offenses, understand the destructive

effects of bitterness, and practice Spirit-led forgiveness and healing.

Preparation for Leaders

- Pray for participants to experience emotional safety, insight, and courage to face past wounds.
- Review Hebrews 12:15, Ephesians 4:31–32, Matthew 17:20.
- Prepare materials: Bibles, journals, pens, optional whiteboard for mapping offenses → forgiveness → healing exercises.

Facilitation Tips

- **Create Emotional Safety:** Participants may revisit painful memories. Encourage pauses, private reflection, and journaling.
- **Encourage Curiosity:** Frame forgiveness as a spiritual and neurological practice—retraining the limbic system through Spirit-led choices.
- **Pacing:** Allow time for reading Scripture, reflecting, journaling, and group discussion.
- **Group Sharing:** Encourage sharing but allow participants to pass if not ready.

Emotional Care & Safety

Why Here?
Unforgiveness and bitterness can fester, affecting emotions, relationships, and even physical health.

Safety Note:
Participants should pause or seek support if emotions become overwhelming. Healing is a process, and God works layer by layer.

Optional Reflection Exercise:

- List one offense you feel ready to release.
- Identify one truth from Scripture that speaks to God's restoration and peace.
- Pray: *"Lord, show me any offense I am holding and help me release it to You today."*

Sample Discussion Questions

- Why is bitterness described as a "root" in Scripture?
- How does unforgiveness poison emotions, relationships, and even the body?
- Which Scripture above gives you the most hope and why?
- How might faith influence your ability to forgive?
- Which offense causes the most emotional pain and how has it shaped your behavior or worldview?

Leader's Encouragement Note

Remind participants:
"Bitterness may have shaped past reactions, but it does not define your future. Every step toward forgiveness is a step toward freedom and healing. God celebrates each surrender of offense."

Optional Add-Ons

- **Worship:** Open with a song about forgiveness, healing, or God's peace.
- **Creative Exercise:** Map offenses → emotional reaction → Scripture truth → Spirit-led response.
- **Testimony Time:** Invite participants to share breakthroughs in releasing resentment or bitterness.

Deliverance Prayers (Optional)

Gentle Prayer:
"Lord, I release all offenses and bitterness that have burdened my heart. Heal my emotions and restore my spirit. Amen."

Authoritative Prayer:
"In the name of Jesus Christ, I renounce all bitterness, resentment, and unforgiveness. I release each person and situation into Your hands. Holy Spirit, replace all offense with Your peace and healing. Amen."

Leader Tip: Before dismissing, encourage participants to complete their daily/weekly activities and journaling prompts. Ask 1–2 volunteers to share insights from the past week to reinforce accountability.

Closing Prayer for Leaders

"Lord, we thank You for Your healing power. Help us release offenses and forgive as You have forgiven us. Restore what has been broken and let Your peace rule in our hearts. In Jesus' name, Amen."

Summary Theme

Releasing bitterness and embracing forgiveness brings healing and lasting rest in God's love.

Section 5 — Soul, Flesh & Spirit

Opening Prayer

God, You know us completely — body, soul, and spirit.
As we explore how You designed us, give us clarity and understanding.
Help us recognize what is driven by emotion or habit, and what is led by Your Spirit.
Teach us how to walk in alignment with Your truth and respond with wisdom.
We invite Your Spirit to lead our thoughts, decisions, and desires.
In Jesus' name, amen.

Section Overview (Leader's Notes)

This section explores the dynamic between the soul, flesh, and Spirit. Leaders guide participants to understand how emotions, will, and mind (soul) interact with the flesh (sinful nature) and the Spirit (prefrontal cortex empowered by the Holy Spirit). Participants learn to identify flesh-driven impulses and practice Spirit-led decision-making, experiencing freedom and transformation.

Key Goal for Participants:
To recognize the influence of flesh and soul on decisions and to cultivate Spirit-led choices that align with God's truth and bring life.

Preparation for Leaders

- Pray for participants to gain discernment, self-awareness, and courage to confront flesh-driven habits.
- Review Romans 8:13, Galatians 5:19–25, Deuteronomy 30:19–20.
- Prepare materials: Bibles, journals, pens, optional chart or whiteboard for mapping flesh vs. Spirit decisions.

Facilitation Tips

- **Create Emotional Safety:** Encourage honest reflection without shame; some may feel convicted or discouraged initially.
- **Encourage Curiosity:** Present the soul/flesh/Spirit model as both biblical truth and scientific insight (limbic system vs. prefrontal cortex).
- **Pacing:** Allow time for Scripture engagement, journaling, discussion, and exercises.
- **Group Sharing:** Invite sharing but normalize passing if participants are not ready.

Emotional Care & Safety

Why Here?
The tension between flesh and Spirit can produce guilt, shame, or confusion. Recognizing the struggle is part of growth, not failure.

Safety Note:
Participants should pause if emotions arise strongly. God works gradually; consistent Spirit-led choices build freedom over time.

Optional Reflection Exercise:

- Identify one habitual reaction or temptation where flesh usually dominates.
- Pray: *"Lord, help me live by Your Spirit today, not my flesh."*

Sample Discussion Questions

- What does Paul contrast in Romans 8:13 between flesh and Spirit?
- How do the emotions and will of the soul interact with the flesh and Spirit?
- Which area of your life is most frequently pulled by the flesh?
- How does understanding the limbic system (emotions, memories) and prefrontal cortex (Spirit-led reasoning) reinforce biblical truth?
- What small step can you take this week to consistently choose Spirit-led decisions?

Leader's Encouragement Note

Remind participants:
"You are not defined by the impulses of your flesh. Every Spirit-led decision strengthens new pathways in your mind and

deepens your identity in Christ. Celebrate small victories along the way."

Optional Add-Ons

- **Worship:** Play music focused on surrender, Spirit-led living, or God's guidance.
- **Creative Exercise:** Chart flesh vs. Spirit decisions in personal situations.
- **Testimony Time:** Invite participants to share a moment of Spirit-led victory over flesh.

Deliverance Prayers (Optional)

Gentle Prayer:
"Holy Spirit, guide me daily in Spirit-led choices. Help me resist fleshly impulses and walk in Your freedom. Amen."

Authoritative Prayer:
"In the name of Jesus, I submit my flesh to Your Spirit. I renounce all ungodly impulses and invite the Spirit to guide every thought, emotion, and decision. Strengthen me to live consistently by Your Spirit. Amen."

Leader Tip: Before dismissing, encourage participants to complete their daily/weekly activities and journaling prompts. Ask 1–2 volunteers to share insights from the past week to reinforce accountability.

Closing Prayer for Leaders

"Lord, thank You for empowering us to live by Your Spirit. Help us resist the pull of the flesh and cultivate Spirit-led choices that bring life, peace, and freedom. In Jesus' name, Amen."

Summary Theme

Walking in the Spirit brings freedom, peace, and rest that the flesh can never give.

Section 6 — The New Man

Opening Prayer

Lord Jesus, thank You for new life.
As we focus on what it means to be born again, help us receive what You have already given us.
Remove old identities, mindsets, and accusations that no longer belong.
Strengthen our confidence in who we are in You and teach us how to live from that place.
We welcome Your transforming work.
In Jesus' name, amen.

Section Overview (Leader's Notes)

This section explores the transformation from the "Old Man" to the "New Man" in Christ. Leaders guide participants to understand the biblical concept of putting off the old self (flesh/limbic system) and putting on the new self (Spirit-led prefrontal cortex). Participants learn practical ways to walk in freedom, righteousness, and holiness as they embrace their identity in Christ.

Key Goal for Participants:
To recognize their new identity in Christ, practice Spirit-led choices, and experience transformation in thought patterns, behaviors, and daily decisions.

Preparation for Leaders

- Pray for participants to experience the reality of their new identity in Christ.
- Review Ephesians 4:22–24, Colossians 3:9–10, Romans 8:5–8.
- Prepare materials: Bibles, journals, pens, optional chart for mapping old man vs. new man habits.

Facilitation Tips

- **Encourage Honest Reflection:** Invite participants to identify old habits or thought patterns without shame.
- **Neuroscience Tie-In:** Explain the Old Man = limbic system (flesh) and New Man = prefrontal cortex (Spirit-led reasoning).
- **Pacing:** Allow adequate time for journaling, exercises, and group discussion.
- **Celebrate Progress:** Highlight small victories and Spirit-led decisions.

Emotional Care & Safety

Why Here?
Confronting old patterns can trigger guilt, shame, or feelings of inadequacy.

Safety Note:
Remind participants that the Spirit empowers change and

growth is gradual. Encourage journaling and prayer for guidance.

Sample Discussion Questions

- What does it practically mean to "put off the old" and "put on the new" in daily life?
- How does understanding the limbic system and prefrontal cortex help you see God's design for transformation?
- Which old habits or thought patterns are hardest to surrender?
- How can Scripture and meditation create renewal in your mind?
- How does embracing the new man give freedom from guilt, shame, and condemnation?

Leader's Encouragement Note

Remind participants:
"The new man in Christ is not a future goal—it's your current reality. Each Spirit-led choice strengthens your mind, renews your heart, and reinforces your identity in Him."

Optional Add-Ons

- **Worship:** Music about renewal, transformation, or new identity in Christ.

- **Creative Exercise:** Map old habits vs. new man responses in personal situations.
- **Testimony Time:** Invite participants to share moments of Spirit-led victory over the old man.

Leader Tip: Before dismissing, encourage participants to complete their daily/weekly activities and journaling prompts. Ask 1–2 volunteers to share insights from the past week to reinforce accountability.

Closing Prayer for Leaders

"Lord, thank You that we are renewed in You. Help us to put off the old man and walk daily in Spirit-led freedom, reflecting Your righteousness and holiness in every choice. Amen."

Summary Theme

Living as the new man means resting in the truth that I am already made new in Christ.

Section 7 — Walk in the Spirit

Opening Prayer

Holy Spirit, we acknowledge You as our guide and helper.
As we learn to walk in step with You, teach us how to listen, respond, and trust.
Quiet the noise of fear and distraction, and sharpen our awareness of Your leading.
Grow in us the fruit that reflects Your character.
We yield this time to You.
In Jesus' name, amen.

Section Overview (Leader's Notes)

This section teaches participants how to yield their thoughts, emotions, and actions to the Holy Spirit, experiencing freedom from fleshly desires while producing the Fruit of the Spirit. Leaders guide participants to notice warning signs ("yellow light" moments) and practice Spirit-led responses in daily life.

Key Goal for Participants:
To recognize flesh-driven impulses, respond with Spirit-led choices, and cultivate a consistent lifestyle of walking in the Spirit.

Preparation for Leaders

- Pray for sensitivity to the Holy Spirit and wisdom to guide participants in practical applications.
- Review Galatians 5:16, 5:25; Romans 12:2; Philippians 4:8.
- Prepare journals, pens, and optional thought-tracking charts.

Facilitation Tips

- **Encourage Reflection:** Ask participants to identify habitual "yellow light" moments in their daily life.
- **Neuroscience Tie-In:** Emphasize how the brain's negativity bias interacts with fleshly impulses and how Scripture retrains thought patterns.
- **Practical Exercises:** Use traffic light analogy to illustrate recognizing Spirit-led vs. flesh-driven responses.
- **Celebrate Small Wins:** Highlight daily or weekly moments of Spirit-led choices.

Emotional Care & Safety

Why Here?
Walking in the Spirit involves confronting negative thought patterns, emotional triggers, or flesh-driven habits.

Safety Note:
Encourage journaling, accountability, and prayer as participants process these challenges without shame.

Sample Discussion Questions

- What does it mean to "walk in the Spirit" in your daily life?
- How do negative thought loops impact your decisions, emotions, and behavior?
- Which fruit of the Spirit is most evident in your life, and which do you desire to grow?
- How can Scripture meditation and thought awareness rewire the mind toward Spirit-led living?
- How does the traffic light analogy help you respond to temptation or warning signs?

Leader's Encouragement Note

Remind participants:
"Walking in the Spirit is not about perfection—it's about awareness and surrender. Each small, Spirit-led choice rewires your mind, strengthens your fruitfulness, and grows your freedom in Christ."

Optional Add-Ons

- **Extended Scripture Meditation:** Spend 10–15 minutes daily meditating on Philippians 4:8, Galatians 5:22-23, or Romans 12:2. Journal insights.
- **Accountability Partner Reflection:** Share daily "yellow light" moments with a trusted friend or mentor for prayer and encouragement.
- **Mindfulness & Breath Practice:** Pause 3–5 minutes daily to breathe and invite the Holy Spirit to guide thoughts and emotions.
- **Fruit of the Spirit Challenge:** Focus on one fruit each week in interactions and track Spirit-led responses.
- **Scripture Memorization:** Commit 1–2 key verses to memory each week to reinforce Spirit-led living.
- **Creative Expression:** Reflect on Spirit-led victories through journaling, poetry, or drawing.
- **Weekly Reflection Circle:** Optional group discussion or virtual meeting to share victories, challenges, and Spirit-led insights.

Prayer & Commitment

Guided Prayer:
"Holy Spirit, I want to walk with You daily. Help me to crucify the desires of my flesh and produce the fruit of the Spirit in my life. Teach me to listen to Your voice and follow Your lead. I surrender my thoughts, my actions, and my will to You. In Jesus' name, Amen."

Personal Commitment:
Invite participants to write their own prayer committing to Spirit-led living.

Closing Prayer for Leaders

"Lord, thank You for teaching us to walk in Your Spirit. Help us notice warning signs, respond with wisdom, and cultivate the Fruit of the Spirit in every area of life. May our daily choices honor You and reflect Your power to transform. Amen."

Summary Theme

Walking in the Spirit is a lifestyle of yielding, where rest is found in trusting His daily guidance.

Section 8 — My Testimony

Opening Prayer

Father, thank You for the power of testimony.
As we reflect on transformation, remind us that You are still writing each story here.
Help us honor one another's journeys and recognize Your grace at work in every stage.
Where there has been brokenness, let hope rise.
Where there has been growth, let gratitude overflow.
In Jesus' name, amen.

Section Overview (Leader's Notes)

This section guides participants to reflect on their life before Christ, the turning point of surrender, and their life after committing to Him. Leaders help participants understand that their testimony carries power—bringing God glory and encouraging others. Participants are equipped to organize, write, and share their story with confidence.

Key Goal for Participants:
To recognize God's redeeming work in their lives, organize their story, and confidently share a testimony that points others to Christ.

Preparation for Leaders:

- Pray for sensitivity to the Holy Spirit and boldness to guide participants in reflecting on personal experiences.
- Review Revelation 12:11; 2 Corinthians 5:17; Philippians 4:13.
- Prepare journals, pens, and optional outlines for organizing testimony.

Facilitation Tips:

- Encourage Reflection: Ask participants to identify significant moments before and after Christ that shaped their story.
- Scripture Tie-In: Highlight verses that affirm God's redemption, transformation, and strength in their testimony.
- Practical Exercises: Use the 3-part framework (Before Christ / How I Met Christ / Life After Christ) for clarity.
- Celebrate Milestones: Acknowledge participants' courage in sharing even small portions of their story.

Emotional Care & Safety

Why Here?
Reflecting on past struggles can bring up emotional wounds or shame. Leaders should guide participants to process with grace.
Safety Note:
Encourage journaling, prayer, and optional one-on-one support.

Remind participants their testimony is valuable regardless of imperfections.

Sample Discussion Questions:

- What was life like before you encountered Christ?
- What moment, person, or scripture led you to surrender your life?
- How has God's intervention transformed your thoughts, actions, and emotions?
- How can sharing your testimony bring hope to others?
- What challenges do you face in expressing your story, and how can Scripture guide your confidence?

Leader's Encouragement Note:

Remind participants:
"Your story is powerful because God redeemed it. You don't need perfection—honesty and reflection are enough. Each testimony shared strengthens faith in yourself and others."

Optional Add-Ons

- **Extended Reflection:** Spend extra time journaling on formative moments or recurring themes in your life.
- **Scripture Meditation:** Choose additional verses that highlight God's redemption and write reflections.
- **Testimony Mapping:** Create a visual timeline of life events showing God's work and guidance.

- **Practice Sharing:** Role-play or record a 3–5 minute version of your testimony.
- **Accountability Partner Feedback:** Share your testimony with a trusted friend and receive encouragement and prayer.
- **Creative Expression:** Write a poem, song, or visual representation inspired by your story.
- **Weekly Reflection Circle:** Optional group discussion to share insights, encouragement, and prayer support.

Prayer & Commitment

Guided Prayer:
"Lord, thank You for redeeming my story. Help me walk in boldness, free from shame, and ready to share my testimony so that others may know You. Use my past for Your glory and let my life point to Jesus. Amen."

Personal Commitment:
Invite participants to write their own prayer committing to live openly in God's redemption and courageously share their testimony.

Leader Tip: Before dismissing, encourage participants to complete their daily/weekly activities and journaling prompts. Ask 1–2 volunteers to share insights from the past week to reinforce accountability.

Closing Prayer for Leaders

"Lord, thank You for guiding each participant in reflecting on their story. Help us all to encourage one another, speak boldly about Your work in our lives, and trust that our testimonies bring glory to You. Amen."

Summary Theme

My testimony is a gift from God—resting in it means trusting Him to use my story for His glory.

Section 9 — A Transformed Heart

Opening Prayer

Lord, give us hearts that are soft, humble, and aligned with You.
As we focus on reverence and obedience, help us understand Your ways more deeply.
Remove fear that drives avoidance and replace it with awe that leads to wisdom.
Shape our hearts to desire what You desire.
We submit this time to You.
In Jesus' name, amen.

Section Overview (Leader's Notes)

This section helps participants understand that lasting transformation requires more than a renewed mind—it requires a heart aligned with God's Spirit. Leaders guide participants to explore fear of the Lord, obedience, and the Spirit's ongoing work, showing how desires, thoughts, and actions can harmonize with God's Kingdom.

Key Goal for Participants:
To recognize areas where the heart resists God's truth, practice obedience, and cultivate a lifestyle where mind, heart, and actions are aligned with the Spirit.

Preparation for Leaders:

- Pray for discernment and sensitivity to participants' emotional and spiritual needs.
- Review Jeremiah 17:9–10; Jeremiah 31:33; Proverbs 9:10; Hebrews 12:28.
- Prepare journals, pens, and optional charts for tracking heart alignment.

Facilitation Tips:

- Encourage Reflection: Ask participants to identify moments where their heart lagged behind their renewed mind.
- Scripture Tie-In: Highlight how God writes His instructions on the heart and transforms desires.
- Practical Exercises: Use daily and weekly exercises to practice obedience in small, tangible ways.
- Celebrate Growth: Highlight instances where following God's Spirit over natural desires brought peace or clarity.

Emotional Care & Safety

Why Here?
Heart-level transformation can surface resistance, shame, or regret from past choices.
Safety Note:
Encourage journaling, prayer, and supportive discussion.

Remind participants that God's work in the heart is progressive and compassionate.

Sample Discussion Questions:

- What does it look like for the heart to resist God's truth even when the mind agrees?
- How would you describe "the fear of the Lord" in your life?
- In what ways have you seen obedience transform your heart's desires?
- What steps can you take to align your daily decisions with God's Spirit?
- How does Scripture guide your heart toward reverence, wisdom, and peace?

Leader's Encouragement Note:

Remind participants:
"Transformation is not instant—it's a process where God rewires desires and aligns your heart with His will. Each obedient choice strengthens your alignment and produces wisdom, peace, and freedom."

Optional Add-Ons

- **Scripture Meditation:** Meditate on Proverbs 9:10, Jeremiah 31:33, or Hebrews 12:28, focusing on heart-level alignment.
- **Obedience Mapping:** Track small daily decisions where you consciously chose God's way over natural desire.
- **Accountability Partner Check-In:** Share heart-alignment challenges with a trusted friend for prayer and encouragement.
- **Creative Expression:** Reflect on heart transformation through art, poetry, or written testimony.
- **Weekly Reflection Circle:** Optional discussion to celebrate obedience milestones and share lessons learned.

Prayer & Commitment

Guided Prayer:
"Father, carve Your Spirit into my heart. Teach me what it truly means to fear You with reverence, awe, and love. Help me to trust You fully, obey You completely, and walk in holiness. Transform my heart so that my desires align with Yours. In Jesus' name, Amen."

Personal Commitment:
Invite participants to write the date and their personal commitment to obey and align their hearts with God's Spirit.

Leader Tip: Before dismissing, encourage participants to complete their daily/weekly activities and journaling prompts. Ask 1–2 volunteers to share insights from the past week to reinforce accountability.

Closing Prayer for Leaders

"Lord, thank You for working in each participant's heart. Help us guide them to notice resistance, practice obedience, and trust Your faithful work. May their desires increasingly align with Your will, producing wisdom, peace, and holiness. Amen."

Summary Theme

A transformed heart rests in God's faithful work of aligning desires, producing obedience, wisdom, and consistent Spirit-led living.

Section 10 — 30, 60, 100 Fold

Opening Prayer

Father, thank You that growth is a journey, not a race.
As we consider maturity and fruitfulness, help us remain faithful in the season we are in.
Guard us from comparison and pride, and lead us instead into perseverance and trust.
Teach us how to steward what You have given and continue pressing forward in You.
We rely on Your strength.
In Jesus' name, amen.

Section Overview (Leader's Notes)

This section frames spiritual growth as a journey in both baptism and temple imagery. Participants are guided to understand spiritual growth as a journey through stages: 30-fold (salvation/water baptism / Outer Court), 60-fold (Spirit empowerment/fire baptism / Holy Place), and 100-fold (daily renewal/air baptism / Throne Room). Leaders help participants explore how these stages connect to obedience, intimacy with God, and pressing forward toward the upward call of God in Christ (Philippians 3:14):

- **30-fold → Water Baptism / Outer Court — salvation, cleansing, repentance, and new birth.**
- **60-fold → Fire Baptism / Holy Place — Spirit empowerment, refining, consecration, and service.**

- **100-fold → Air (Spirit) Baptism / Holy of Holies / Throne Room** — daily renewal, intimacy, union with God's presence, and eternal "Full" reward.

Leaders: Participants will see that the parable of the sower (Mark 4:20), the stages of baptism, and the temple pattern are unified pictures of pressing forward toward maturity in Christ.

Key Goal for Participants:
To locate themselves within the 30-60-100 fold journey, recognize God's invitation to deeper stages, and commit to daily Spirit-led practices that move them toward intimacy in the Throne Room.

Preparation for Leaders

- Pray for discernment to help participants see growth without comparison or condemnation.
- Review core Scriptures: Mark 4:20, Philippians 3:13–14, Romans 6:3–4, Acts 2:1–4, Hebrews 9:6–7, Romans 8:13.
- Familiarize yourself with the temple structure (Outer Court, Holy Place, Holy of Holies) and how it parallels the 30-60-100 fold stages.
- Prepare journals, pens, and optional visuals: a three-circle diagram (court → place → holies) or a fold chart.

Facilitation Tips

- Layered Teaching: Present the baptism progression first, then introduce the temple imagery as a deeper layer.
- Invitation, Not Pressure: Frame 30-fold, 60-fold, and 100-fold as progressive invitations, not performance requirements.
- Allow participants to locate themselves gently in this framework; this is an invitation to intimacy with God, not a measure of spiritual maturity.
- Scripture Tie-In: Show how water, fire, and Spirit imagery connects to the stages of the temple and the believer's walk.
- Practical Practices: Encourage journaling, communion, prayer in the Spirit, and intimacy practices aligned with each stage.
- Celebrate Faithfulness: Emphasize that God honors even small, faithful steps of growth.

Emotional Care & Safety

Why Here?
As participants reflect on their spiritual stage, some may feel inadequate, ashamed, or pressured.

Safety Note:

- Emphasize grace: growth happens in God's timing.
- Encourage journaling and private reflection before sharing.
- Remind them that no stage is "less loved" — God honors faithfulness.

The Temple–Baptism Framework (Leader's Teaching)

Stage	Baptism Expression	Temple Imagery	Meaning for Believers	Key Scriptures
30-Fold	Water Baptism	Outer Court	Cleansing, repentance, salvation; beginning of the journey	Romans 6:3–4; John 3:5
60-Fold	Fire Baptism	Holy Place	Refining, consecration, Spirit empowerment, service	Acts 2:1–4; Malachi 3:2–3
100-Fold	Air Baptism	Holy of Holies / Throne Room	Daily renewal, intimacy with God, union with His presence, eternal reward	Hebrews 9:6–7; Rev. 4:1–2

Sample Discussion Questions

- How does the Outer Court / Holy Place / Holy of Holies progression deepen your understanding of 30-60-100 fold growth?
- What connections do you see between baptism (water, fire, Spirit) and temple stages?
- Which stage do you feel you're in now? What practices could help you "press forward"?
- How does Paul's pressing forward (Phil. 3:13–14) encourage you not to stay at one fold but pursue intimacy with God?

Optional Add-Ons for Leaders

- Visual Teaching: Draw the temple or use a diagram to show progression.
- Extended Reflection: Have participants journal about how they experience God in each "stage."
- Scripture Meditation: Encourage meditation on Hebrews 10:19–22 about entering the Holy of Holies.
- Group Sharing: Create a "fold circle" where participants share a practice they are using to grow.
- Creative Practice: Invite them to write a psalm, prayer, or sketch that reflects their growth journey.

Leader's Encouragement Note

"The 30-60-100 fold journey is not about comparison, but about pressing forward into God's invitation. Each stage carries beauty: the cleansing of salvation, the fire of consecration, and the intimacy of the Throne Room. Encourage participants to honor the stage they're in while reaching forward in hope."

Prayer & Commitment

Guided Prayer:
"Lord, I thank You for calling me deeper. I receive the cleansing of water, the refining of fire, and the intimacy of Your Spirit. Lead me from the Outer Court, into the Holy Place, and into the Throne Room, where I may dwell with You. Teach me to press forward every day toward Your upward call. Amen."

Personal Commitment:
Invite participants to write their own prayer or declaration of pressing forward through the 30-60-100 fold stages.

Closing Prayer for Leaders

"Father, thank You for guiding this group through the stages of growth. May each participant find joy in salvation, strength in consecration, and intimacy in Your presence. Teach us to press on toward the prize of knowing You fully, and may our lives bear 30, 60, and 100-fold fruit for Your glory. Amen."

Summary Theme

Spiritual growth is both progression through baptismal stages (water, fire, Spirit) and movement into God's dwelling places (Outer Court, Holy Place, Holy of Holies). The journey presses believers into deeper intimacy with Christ and prepares them for eternal fellowship in the Throne Room.

Extending the Journey: The Secret Place Within Ecosystem

This Leader's Guide is part of a broader discipleship ecosystem created by **4Given Life - Music Ministries** to support churches, leaders, and facilitators as they guide individuals and groups toward renewed minds, transformed hearts, and Spirit-led living.

While this guide and its accompanying workbook are designed to stand complete on their own, The Secret Place Within ecosystem provides optional resources that help extend and support the journey beyond the pages of this book. These tools are offered to strengthen consistency, care, and clarity as churches steward discipleship, healing, and growth within their local context.

Additional Resources Available

Through the 4Given Life website, leaders may access supplemental materials that support and enhance this study, including:

- Certificates of completion
- Facilitator support materials
- Optional group handouts
- Supplemental teaching and reflection resources
- Updates and future training opportunities

These resources are designed to serve leaders and churches with flexibility while maintaining alignment with the principles of emotional safety, grace-centered growth, and Spirit-led discipleship outlined in this guide.

How to Access the Ecosystem

To view the full *The Secret Place Within* ecosystem and available downloads, visit:

www.4givenlife-musicministries.com

Navigate to the "The Secret Place Within" tab to access resources connected to this study.

A Word of Discernment

The resources within this ecosystem are intended to support—not replace—prayerful leadership, pastoral oversight, and the guidance of the Holy Spirit. Churches and leaders are encouraged to engage these materials in ways that honor their local context while upholding the emotional-care and safety principles presented throughout this Leader's Guide.

This journey does not end here. The tools provided—both within this book and beyond it—are meant to help leaders cultivate environments where transformation can continue to unfold with wisdom, patience, and grace.

Final Conclusion — No Longer a Secret Place

Opening Prayer

Father God, we thank You for the work You have done and for the work You will continue to do.
As we come to this concluding section, help us reflect with gratitude, humility, and hope.
Reveal what You have strengthened, healed, and begun to transform in each of us.
Where there is still growth ahead, grant patience and trust in Your timing.
Seal what has been learned, guard what has been restored, and guide each step forward.
We place what comes next in Your hands, confident that You are faithful to complete what You started.
In Jesus' name, amen.

Section Overview (Leader's Notes)

This final section guides participants to bring God's light into the hidden areas of their lives—places once filled with sin, shame, guilt, or brokenness. Leaders help participants reflect on how science and Scripture worked together to renew their minds, and how surrendering these "secret places" to God brings lasting freedom, transformation, and empowerment to walk as children of light.

Key Goal for Participants:
To recognize God's light in previously hidden areas, embrace ongoing transformation, and commit to a daily life of freedom, surrender, and Spirit-led living.

Preparation for Leaders:

- Pray for discernment, sensitivity, and celebration of participants' growth.
- Review Ephesians 5:8, Isaiah 9:6, Psalm 147:3, Romans 12:2, James 5:16.
- Prepare journals, pens, and optional reflection charts.

Facilitation Tips:

- Encourage Reflection: Invite participants to identify areas where God's light is already working in their lives.
- Scripture Tie-In: Reinforce the connection between biblical truths and practical, science-informed strategies for mind renewal.
- Practical Exercises: Use journaling, verbal declarations, or sharing testimonies to cement transformation.
- Celebrate Milestones: Acknowledge breakthroughs and progress, both visible and internal.

Emotional Care & Safety

Why Here?
Revealing "secret places" can bring strong emotions, guilt, or shame.
Safety Note:
Encourage participants to approach journaling, reflection, and sharing at their own pace. Emphasize accountability, prayer, and grace-filled community support.

Sample Discussion Questions:

- Where has God's light begun to shine in your "secret place"?
- How do Scripture and science work together to help you process and transform your life?
- What does it mean to walk daily as a child of light?
- How has surrendering hidden areas to God produced freedom or healing?
- Which practices from the workbook will you continue to maintain lasting transformation?

Leader's Encouragement Note:

Remind participants:
"God honors your willingness to bring hidden areas into the light. Transformation is ongoing, but your identity in Christ is secure. Every step of surrender produces freedom, peace, and joy."

Optional Add-Ons

- **Extended Reflection:** Spend 10–15 minutes each day reviewing past journal entries to see God's progress.
- **Testimony Sharing:** Share breakthroughs with a trusted friend, mentor, or small group.
- **Daily Light Declaration:** Each morning, speak over your life: "Lord, shine Your light into every hidden corner of my heart."
- **Scripture Memorization:** Commit key verses to memory that remind you of your new identity and freedom.
- **Creative Expression:** Reflect through art, poetry, or music on how God's light has transformed your life.
- **Weekly Celebration Circle:** Optional group or virtual gathering to celebrate freedom, breakthroughs, and growth.

Prayer & Commitment

Guided Prayer:
"Lord, thank You for shining Your light into the hidden places of my heart. I no longer want to keep secrets from You. Fill every corner of my life with Your Spirit, Your truth, and Your freedom. Help me to walk daily as a child of light. Amen."

Personal Commitment:
Invite participants to write their own prayer committing to daily surrender, light-filled living, and continued growth in Christ.

Closing Prayer for Leaders

"Father, thank You for guiding each participant through this journey. Help us encourage them to walk as children of light, living fully in Your truth, and reflecting Your glory. May the breakthroughs and freedom they experienced continue to grow as they trust in You. Amen."

Summary Theme

The journey culminates in freedom—God's light transforms hidden places, renewing mind, heart, and life. Participants are called to walk daily as fully known, fully loved, and fully free children of God.

The Journey's End — Wrap-Up & Stepping Forward in the Spirit

Section Overview (Leader's Notes)

This final wrap-up guides participants to review their progress, celebrate growth, and step forward in Spirit-led living. Leaders encourage reflection on lessons learned, reinforce accountability, and help participants establish ongoing habits for spiritual maturity and freedom.

Key Goal for Participants:
To consolidate the journey, recognize areas of growth, commit to ongoing Spirit-led practices, and establish a support network for accountability and continued transformation.

Final Checklist – Walking It Out

Take a moment to review your journey and mark what you've begun practicing:

- ☐ I understand the difference between flesh-led and Spirit-led living.
- ☐ I can identify when my limbic system (flesh) is driving my decisions.
- ☐ I know how to renew my mind through Scripture, prayer, and reflection.
- ☐ I have practiced replacing false beliefs with God's truth.

- ☐ I can explain what it means to be born again and to "put on the new man."
- ☐ I have recognized at least one area of past struggle and surrendered it to God.
- ☐ I have experienced the Holy Spirit's power helping me choose life over sin.
- ☐ I've begun journaling or reflecting regularly to track my growth.
- ☐ I've taken a step to share my story/testimony with someone else.

Encouragement for the Journey Ahead

- Transformation is not instant—it is daily renewal.
- Temptations may still come, but now you are equipped with truth + Spirit power.
- Remember: willpower is fail power—victory comes only through the Holy Spirit.
- You are not walking alone. God's Spirit, God's Word, and God's people are with you.
- Every small step in obedience is a huge victory in eternity's eyes.

S.T.A.N.D — Support Team Accountability Network Defense

The Group Leader can look at each participant's book to see if they have this filled out. Explain the extreme importance of having this support team set up and

encourage the participants to continue maintaining communication with their S.T.A.N.D

Connect with an accountability partner or spiritual mentor: _____

Pastor: _____
Church: _____
Study Group: _____
Recovery Group: _____
Recovery Sponsor: _____
Therapist/Counselor: _____

Optional Add-Ons

- **Extended Reflection:** Don't forget to spend 10–15 minutes each day or weekly, reviewing past journal entries to see God's progress.
- **Individual Prayer:** Leader may use anointing oil or lay hands (only with participants approval). Pray for the participant with the group surrounding you both.

Leader's Encouragement Note

Remind participants:
"You have completed this journey, but the walk continues. Daily Spirit-led choices, accountability, and reflection will keep your mind, heart, and life aligned with God's truth. Celebrate your growth, rely on the Spirit, and step forward in confidence and freedom."

Closing Prayer

"Lord, thank You for walking with me through this journey. Help me continue to live in Spirit-led freedom, remain in Your Word, and rely on Your power each day. Surround me with a support network, guide my steps, and empower me to walk boldly as Your child. Amen."

Summary Theme

The journey concludes with celebration, reflection, and a commitment to ongoing renewal in the Spirit. Walking forward requires daily obedience, accountability, and reliance on God's truth and power.

Celebration:

Allow a few minutes for participants to share a "Freedom Moment" or celebration testimony. This helps reinforce breakthroughs and ends the course on a note of encouragement, gratitude and praise.

- **Reminder for Leaders:** Your role is to facilitate discussion and encouragement, not to counsel or diagnose. Encourage participants to seek professional help when needed. These tools are provided for your use in good faith; how you apply them is your responsibility. The author and publisher assume no liability for outcomes.

Congratulations! Thank you for your commitment to leading your group on this transformational journey towards inner healing, deliverance, freedom and enhanced spiritual walk with God. Though you have certainly reached a destination, it's not the final destination. My prayer for you is to continue pressing forward in your daily "third expression of Air Baptism" drawing yourself closer to God each and every day. That you would attach closely and addict yourself to the ministry of the saints.

Be well, blessed and "Very Good,"

Craig D. Jemmott
Founder of: 4Given Life – Music Ministries
www.4givenlife-musicministries.com
Tucson, Arizona

To God be the Glory!

Scan this QR code to go directly to
www.4givenlife-musicministries.com

www.ingramcontent.com/pod-product-compliance
Lightning Source LLC
Chambersburg PA
CBHW071203090426
42736CB00012B/2427